Tea Bag Folding
THROUGH THE SEASONS™

Annie's Attic®

Tea Bag Folding
THROUGH THE SEASONS™

EDITOR Tanya Fox
ART DIRECTOR Brad Snow
PUBLISHING SERVICES DIRECTOR Brenda Gallmeyer
ASSOCIATE EDITOR Brooke Smith
ASSISTANT ART DIRECTOR Nick Pierce
COPY SUPERVISOR Deborah Morgan
COPY EDITORS Emily Carter, Mary O'Donnell
TECHNICAL EDITOR Corene Painter
TECHNICAL ARTIST Debera Kuntz
PHOTOGRAPHY SUPERVISOR Tammy Christian
PHOTO STYLISTS Tammy Liechty, Tammy Steiner
PHOTOGRAPHY Matthew Owen
PRODUCTION ARTIST SUPERVISOR Erin Augsburger
GRAPHIC ARTIST Nicole Gage
PRODUCTION ASSISTANTS Marj Morgan, Judy Neuenschwander

ISBN: 978-1-59635-360-2
Printed in the USA
1 2 3 4 5 6 7 8 9

Every effort has been made to ensure that the instructions in this publication are complete and accurate. We cannot, however, take responsibility for human error, typographical mistakes or variations in individual work. Please visit AnniesCustomerCare.com to check for pattern updates.

Contents

Tea-bag folding ... it's a wonderful paper-crafting technique. Partner this technique with card making and you have the perfect combination.

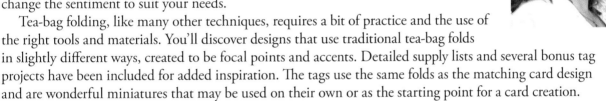

Tea Bag Folding is a collection of card designs that will take you through the entire year with designs that are perfect for any occasion. Some of the designs, such as the Pocket Wishes card on page 26, are for specific occasions. This birthday card could easily be changed into a wedding card by using the bride and groom's initials and by changing the greeting on the tag. It would also make a delightful baby card or shower invitation with only a few simple design modifications. Even if the greeting on a particular card doesn't fit your occasion, take another look as the design itself may be perfect. Simply change the sentiment to suit your needs.

Tea-bag folding, like many other techniques, requires a bit of practice and the use of the right tools and materials. You'll discover designs that use traditional tea-bag folds in slightly different ways, created to be focal points and accents. Detailed supply lists and several bonus tag projects have been included for added inspiration. The tags use the same folds as the matching card design and are wonderful miniatures that may be used on their own or as the starting point for a card creation.

Tea Bag Folding not only shares the how-to on tea-bag folding, but also provides you with complete project instructions, color photos and easy-to-follow folding diagrams. Many popular card-making products have been combined with tea-bag folding to not only show you the applications in which this technique may be used, but also the different products and tools that can be used to complement this technique. My heartfelt thanks go out to the team at Spellbinders™ Paper Arts for not only creating wonderful products, but also for providing product support for this book.

Designing the projects in this book was the perfect opportunity for me to explore this beautiful technique further and to push the envelope, so to speak. I hope you enjoy the results of my journey.

Creatively yours,
Sharon Reinhart

Introduction to Tea-Bag Folding

Tea-bag folding is a paper-crafting technique which traditionally involves the folding of squares of lightweight paper to create medallions or rosettes. Sometimes this technique is referred to as miniature kaleidoscope origami. It is said to have originated in Holland by a woman named Tiny Van Der Plaas, who used the printed papers from tea-bag envelopes or sachets to create her designs. These papers, being lightweight and decorative, worked perfectly. In North America, these pretty tea-bag envelopes are not available, so the art of tea-bag folding has evolved into using a variety of papers. Lightweight scrapbook papers, gift wrap, Chiyogami and origami papers are some of the papers being used.

Papers may also be created with the use of rubber stamps and stencils. Simply apply ink to the stamp and press the image onto lightweight stationery, scrapbook paper or even photocopy paper; cut out and then let the folding and fun begin. Several rubber-stamp companies have created rubber stamps specifically for use with tea-bag folding, and many others have designs that, although they were not created specifically for this technique, offer beautiful results when used. Turn projects "green"

by recycling old security envelopes, use the pattern on the envelope or find a bold image and stamp on top. Then punch or cut into shapes to fold.

There are also printed tea-bag–folding papers available from a variety of manufacturers. The Internet is one further option. Tea-bag tile designs in an assortment of patterns and colors are available to download and print from a computer.

At one time, the shapes typically used were 1½-inch to 2-inch squares of paper. However, with the variety of punches and dies on the market today, beautiful results are being achieved with many different shapes, such as circles, scalloped circles and octagons. Popular shapes, such as the label dies being used in card crafting today, work beautifully, as seen in the Mom card on page 8.

Traditional tea-bag–folded designs result in beautiful medallions and rosettes. As experimenting continues with this technique, more designs are being created and used in a variety of applications. A simple fold can easily become a beautiful corner adornment. Or by assembling the traditional folded pieces in a slightly different manner, a dimensional rectangle can be brought to life. Butterflies, umbrellas and even flowers are all possible to create with just a few folded shapes. Once the fundamental folds have been learned, a foundation has been established to go above and beyond just the basics.

The keys to success with this technique are creating precise folds, sharp creases and using the right materials and tools. And remember, as with anything good in life, practice does make perfect. To create the actual folded pieces, there are a few tools that will help ensure a smooth process. A paper trimmer, scissors, adhesives—including a glue

stick and double-sided tape—and a bone folder are items that should be added to your paper-crafting tool kit if not already included (see Photo 1). A bone folder is not only useful in scoring your base card to fold in half but also for burnishing over the folds to make sharp creases. Using the bone folder rather than your fingernail will offer a more professional look in the finished piece.

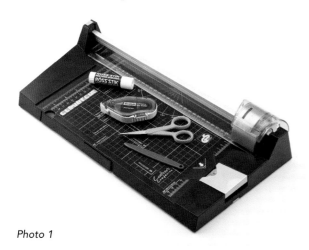

Photo 1

For adhesive purposes, it is good to have a variety on hand; the two mentioned earlier are a minimum. Additional products to consider are adhesive dots, glue pen and various styles of tape runners. Experimenting with different adhesives will help determine which work the best for you.

A paper-crafting tool kit is essential, not only for the actual completion of projects, but also to help make crafting a pleasant experience. Each person has a slightly different tool kit which changes and evolves over time. Items considered to be part of a basic paper-crafting kit are: a paper trimmer, scissors, metal-edge ruler, embossing stylus, piercing tool and mat, bone folder, pliers/tweezers, a variety of adhesives and a pencil. A notebook is always useful for recording information or for that next creative idea.

Basic Folds

Three folds that are commonly used for tea-bag folding are the Basic Triangle Fold, Basic Square Fold and Basic Circle Fold. These may be used as is, or they can be built upon for more intricate folds.

Basic Triangle Fold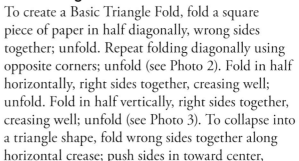

To create a Basic Triangle Fold, fold a square piece of paper in half diagonally, wrong sides together; unfold. Repeat folding diagonally using opposite corners; unfold (see Photo 2). Fold in half horizontally, right sides together, creasing well; unfold. Fold in half vertically, right sides together, creasing well; unfold (see Photo 3). To collapse into a triangle shape, fold wrong sides together along horizontal crease; push sides in toward center, pushing along horizontal fold (see Photo 4).

Photo 2

Photo 3

Photo 4

Basic Square Fold

To create a Basic Square Fold, fold a square piece of paper in half horizontally, wrong sides together; unfold. Fold in half vertically, wrong sides together; unfold (see Photo 5). Fold in half diagonally in one direction, right sides together, creasing well; unfold. Fold in half diagonally in the opposite corners, right sides together, creasing well; unfold (see Photo 6). To collapse into a square shape on angle, fold wrong sides together along one of the diagonal creases, push sides in toward center, pushing along diagonal fold (see Photo 7).

Basic Circle Fold

This fold is a variation of the Basic Square Fold. When folding circles, there is a slight variation due to the shape.

To create a Basic Circle Fold, fold a circular piece of paper in half horizontally, wrong sides together; do not unfold. Fold piece in half vertically, creating a pie-shaped piece (see Photo 8). Unfold all. Fold circle in half one more time, rotating circle so fold will intersect where previous two folds meet at center of circle; do not unfold (see Photo 9). To collapse into a pie shape, push sides in toward center, pushing along last folded line (see Photo 10).

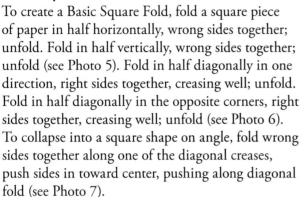

Photo 5

Photo 8

Photo 6

Photo 9

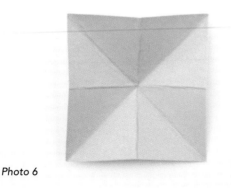

Photo 7

Photo 10

Beyond Basic Folds

From these basic folds or foundations, an infinite number of designs may be created. The basic folds can be assembled as is to create medallions and rosettes, or with just a couple additional folds, the design may be totally changed. Often, when adding the additional folds, the top or bottom layers are folded into the center fold. As shown in the photos, both a basic folded triangle and square consist of a top layer and a bottom layer. They are joined together by the center fold that runs through the middle. The center fold is the fold which is pressed on in order to collapse the shape into either a triangle or square. If the paper is not even to begin with and a small amount of white space is peeking out of the folded shape, simply trim it off. If the shape is not symmetrical once it is folded, it is best to redo it, as it will affect the final shape once assembled.

The center portion of an assembled medallion may have a specific design resembling a flower, kaleidoscope, geometric or graphic design. It may have been completed simply to accentuate the dimension of the folds. This depends totally on the paper being used and on how the squares are being folded. When trying to recreate a center picture, geometric or graphic design, be sure to stay consistent with the folds created for each shape.

Tea-bag–folded medallions are the perfect surfaces for adding embellishments. A pearl brad, rhinestone, flower or a button can serve as a beautiful finishing touch. Whereas, some designs are absolutely perfect with the "less is more" approach.

Squash Fold

A squash fold, believed to be borrowed from the origami world, is an extra fold created on an already folded piece.

With the fold line facing up, fold one tip of top layer over, aligning straight outside edges (see Photo 11); unfold. Insert toothpick or unfolded paperclip into the inside space of top layer (see Photo 12). Using your fingers, press along the original fold "squashing" it down onto the surface (see Photo 13).

This will create a squash fold (see Photo 14). *Note: Squash folds can be done on the top or bottom layer of a folded piece.*

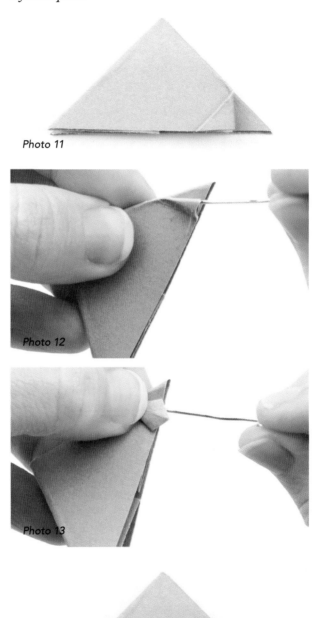

Photo 11

Photo 12

Photo 13

Photo 14

Now that you have the foundation techniques, let the tea-bag folding begin! ∎

Mom

Materials

- Card stock: lime green, pale pink
- Gossamer Collection SC-Flitter printed paper
- Pale pink text-weight paper
- Narratives® Circle Uppercase Alphabet Stamp set
- Lime green dye ink pad
- Large silver brad
- Circle punches: ⅝-inch, ¾-inch
- Die templates: Labels One (#S4-161), Standard Circles SM (#S4-116)
- Die-cutting machine
- Paper piercer
- Adhesive foam tape
- Double-sided tape
- Paper adhesive

Project note: Use paper adhesive throughout unless otherwise instructed.

Form a 5½ x 5½-inch top-folded card from SC-Flitter paper.

Using 1⅞-inch Labels One die template, die-cut eight labels from pale pink paper and one from lime green card stock. Fold each label into a triangle referring to Basic Triangle Fold instructions on page 5. Ink curved outer edges of each pink triangle. Set lime green triangle aside.

To assemble floral medallion, place a small piece of double-sided tape onto back left corner of each pink triangle. Slip top layer of one pink triangle under top layer of another pink triangle. Referring to Fig. 1–3, continue working around until floral medallion is complete.

Punch a ¾-inch circle from lime green card stock; adhere to brad. Pierce a hole through center of floral medallion and center of card front. Insert brad through center of medallion and then through card front, securing medallion to card. Using two largest Standard Circles SM die templates, die-cut a ring from lime green card stock. Adhere ring to card front around medallion.

Stamp "MOM" onto pale pink card stock. Using ⅝-inch circle punch, punch out each letter. Adhere "MOM" to card front as shown using foam tape.

Cut lime green triangle in half between layers. *Note: Triangle can be unfolded before cutting. Cut along horizontal fold. Then refold each piece to create two photo corners.* Slide photo corners onto bottom corners of card front and adhere in place. ∎

Sources: Printed paper from Memory Box; stamp set from Creative Imaginations; circle punches from EK Success; die templates from Spellbinders™ Paper Arts; die-cutting machine from Sizzix.

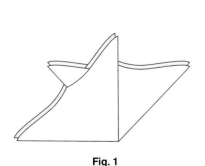

Fig. 1

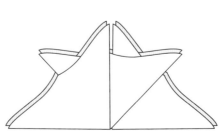

Fig. 2

Fig. 3

Love

Materials

- Card stock: white, black
- Black/white floral printed paper
- "Love" background image stamp
- Black dye ink pad
- 2 large black circle brads
- Small clear self-adhesive gem
- Punches: Dotted Wave Edger,
  1-inch circle, 2-inch circle
- Die templates: Classic Scalloped
  Circles SM (#S4-125), Decorative
  Flourishes Set (#656538)
- Embossed Tags embossing folder
  (#20-00250)
- Die-cutting and embossing
  machine
- Paper piercer
- Scoring tool
- Adhesive foam tape
- Double-sided tape
- Paper adhesive
- Computer with printer (optional)

Project note: *Use paper adhesive throughout unless otherwise instructed.*

Card

Cut 7½ x 5½-inch piece from white card stock. With long edge horizontal, score a vertical line 3¼ inches from left side. Fold at score line to create a side-folded card with a 3¼-inch-wide card front. Adhere a 3¼ x 5½-inch piece of printed paper to card front.

Cut a 1⅝ x 5½-inch piece from black card stock. Punch one long edge using Dotted Wave Edger punch. Adhere to back of right edge on card front as shown.

Stamp "Love" background onto white card stock. *Note: If "Love" background stamp is unavailable, use a computer and printer to generate "Love" multiple times onto white card stock.* Using 1-inch circle punch, punch a circle from stamped area. Set aside.

Using Classic Scalloped Circles SM die templates, die-cut a 1⅜-inch circle and a 2⅜-inch circle from black card stock. Adhere stamped circle to 1⅜-inch scalloped circle. Attach self-adhesive gem to the "o" in one "Love." Adhere to lower right corner of card front as shown. Set 2⅜-inch scalloped circle aside.

Punch eight 2-inch circles from printed paper. Fold each circle referring to Basic Circle Fold instructions on page 6.

To complete each folded circle, fold top right layer over and toward center fold, aligning outside right edge with center fold (Fig. 1). Repeat fold with top left layer (Fig. 2). Repeat process with all folded circles.

To assemble rosette, apply a small piece of double-sided tape to back left corner of each folded circle. Slip bottom layer of one folded circle under top layer of another folded circle (Fig. 3). Continue working around until rosette is complete (Fig. 4 and 5). To secure rosette, adhere it to 2⅜-inch die-cut scalloped circle.

Pierce a hole through center of rosette; insert brad.

Using Decorative Flourish die template, die-cut two flourishes from black card stock. Adhere flourishes to back of rosette. Referring to photo, adhere rosette with flourishes to card front.

Tag

Using Embossed Tags embossing folder, die-cut a tag from white card stock. Adhere printed paper to front of tag; trim edges flush with die-cut tag.

Punch one 2-inch circle from black card stock and four circles from printed paper. Set black circle aside.

Referring to card-making instructions, fold printed paper circles.

To assemble tag rosette, slip bottom layer of one folded circle under top layer of another folded circle (Fig. 3). Repeat with remaining two folded circles.

Adhere double-folded circles across from each other on black circle. Pierce a hole through center of rosette; insert brad.

Adhere to tag as shown. ■

Sources: Printed paper from Michaels Stores Inc.; Dotted Wave Edger punch from EK Success; circle punches from Marvy Uchida; Classic Scalloped Circles SM die templates from Spellbinders™ Paper Arts; Decorative Flourishes Set, and die-cutting and embossing machine from Sizzix; Cuttlebug embossing folder from Provo Craft.

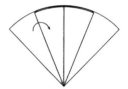

Fig. 1

Fig. 2

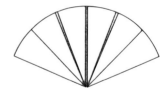

Fig. 3

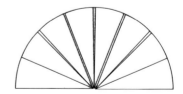

Fig. 4

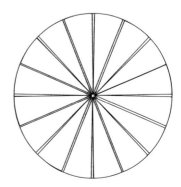

Fig. 5

Just Because

Materials

- Card stock: pink pearlescent, sage green, white
- Green floral printed paper
- Pink thread
- White decorative button
- Southwest corner punch
- Embossing folders: Embossed Tags (#20-00250), Diamond (#656796)
- Die-cutting and embossing machine
- Scoring tool
- Toothpick
- Double-sided tape
- Tape
- Paper adhesive

Project note: *Use paper adhesive throughout unless otherwise instructed.*

Card

Cut an 8½ x 5½-inch piece from pink pearlescent card stock. With long edge horizontal on work surface, score vertical lines 2⅛ inches and 6⅜ inches from left edge. Fold at scored lines to form a 4¼ x 5½-inch gatefold card. Using Diamond embossing folder, emboss both front panels of card front.

Cut two 2⅞ x 2⅞-inch squares from sage green card stock, set one square aside. Adhere one square centered to card front, adhering it to right panel as shown.

Cut a 2⅜ x 2⅜-inch square from white card stock. Punch all four corners using Southwest corner punch. Wrap pink thread around each corner and across white square as shown; secure ends to back. Center and adhere thread-wrapped square to sage green square on card front.

Cut four 2-inch squares from green floral paper. Fold each square referring to Basic Triangle Fold instructions on page 5. Secure bottom layer of folded triangle with double-sided tape.

To complete each folded triangle, fold right top layer over, aligning outside edge with center fold (Fig. 1). Repeat with left top layer (Fig. 2). Referring to Squash Fold instructions on page 7, squash-fold both folded edges (Fig. 3 and 4).

Referring to Fig. 5 and 6 for placement, assemble rosette using four folded pieces, placing folded pieces right side facedown on work surface. Aligning straight edges, attach folded pieces together with tape. ***Note:*** *For added security, adhere a small square of card stock to back of rosette.* Adhere assembled rosette to card front as shown. Adhere button to center of rosette.

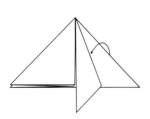

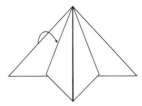
Squash Fold

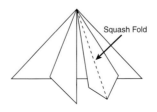

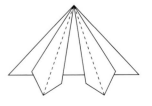

| **Fig. 1** | **Fig. 2** | **Fig. 3** | **Fig. 4** |

Tag

Using Embossed Tags embossing folder, die-cut and emboss a tag from pink pearlescent card stock. Die-cut tag hole cover from sage green card stock. Adhere tag hole cover to tag.

Cut a 1⅜ x 1⅜-inch piece from sage green card stock and a 1⅛ x 1⅛-inch piece from white card stock. Layer and adhere to tag as shown.

Cut two 1½ x 1½-inch squares from green floral paper. Referring to folding instructions from card instructions, create two folded pieces. Adhere folded pieces to tag front as shown. ∎

Sources: Card stock from Bazzill Basics Paper Inc.; printed paper from Michaels Stores Inc.; Southwest corner punch from Marvy Uchida; Cuttlebug Embossed Tags embossing folder from Provo Craft; Diamond embossing folder, and Big Shot die-cutting and embossing machine from Sizzix.

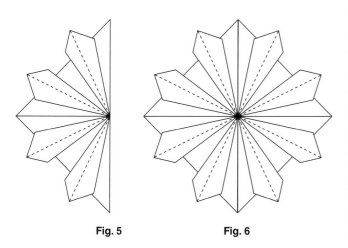

Fig. 5   **Fig. 6**

Happy Easter

Project note: *Use paper adhesive throughout unless otherwise instructed.*

Card

Form a 5½ x 5½-inch side-folded card from lavender pearlescent card stock.

Using 4 x 4-inch Eyelet Squares die template, die-cut and emboss two squares from white pearlescent paper. Set one square aside.

Cut ribbon into four 4-inch lengths. Referring to photo, insert ends of one length of ribbon through holes at corner of eyelet square; cross ribbon ends over on back and insert ribbon ends through opposite holes to return to front. Repeat on remaining corners. Adhere to card front.

Using 3-inch Eyelet Circles die template, die-cut and emboss a circle from lavender pearlescent card stock. Adhere to card front as shown.

Stamp Heart Blossom Square eight times onto white pearlescent paper. Heat-set ink with embossing heat tool. Cut out stamped squares. Fold each square referring to Basic Triangle Fold instructions on page 5. Once folded, trim around curved edge of stamped image (Fig. 1).

To assemble rosette, apply a small piece of double-sided tape to back left corner of each folded piece. Slip top layer of one folded triangle under top layer of another folded triangle (Fig. 2). Continue working around until circle is complete (Fig. 3 and 4).

Pierce hole through center of rosette; insert brad. Adhere to card front as shown. Attach rhinestone flower to brad.

Stamp "Happy Easter" onto remaining die-cut square; heat-set ink. Adhere inside card.

Tag

Die-cut a 3-inch Eyelet Circle from lavender pearlescent card stock.

Stamp Heart Blossom Square four times onto white pearlescent paper; heat-set ink. Cut out each stamped square.

Fold in the same manner as card instructions.

Referring to photo, adhere folded pieces to die-cut circle, aligning straight edges. Pierce a hole through center of folded pieces; insert brad. Attach rhinestone flower to brad. Punch a 1½-inch circle from lavender pearlescent card stock; adhere to back of tag to cover brad. ∎

Sources: Card stock and paper from ANW Crestwood/The Paper Company; Heart Blossom Square stamp from Inkadinkado; A Very Happy Easter stamp from Penny Black Inc.; die templates from Spellbinders™ Paper Arts; die-cutting and embossing machine from Sizzix.

Materials
- Lavender pearlescent card stock
- White pearlescent paper
- Stamps: Heart Blossom Square, A Very Happy Easter (#4038F)
- Lavender ink pad
- 2 lavender self-adhesive rhinestone flowers
- 2 white round brads
- 16 inches ¼-inch-wide lavender sheer ribbon
- 1½-inch circle punch
- Die templates: Eyelet Circles (#S4-304), Eyelet Squares (#S4-305)
- Die-cutting and embossing machine
- Embossing heat tool
- Paper piercer
- Double-sided tape
- Paper adhesive

Fig. 1

Fig. 2

Fig. 3

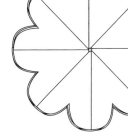

Fig. 4

Happy Birthday

Project notes: *Use paper adhesive throughout unless otherwise instructed. This medallion consists of a double fold, whereby the front and back of each piece is folded.*

Form a 5½ x 4¼-inch top-folded card from light teal linen card stock.

Using Apron Lace border punch, punch top and bottom edges of a 5½ x 1¼-inch strip of white card stock. Center and adhere to card front. Wrap ribbon around card front over punched strip; tie knot on right side and trim ends.

Stamp "happy birthday" onto white card stock. Cut a small rectangle around sentiment; adhere to lower right area of card front.

Cut eight 2-inch squares from floral paper. Fold each square referring to Basic Triangle Fold instructions on page 5.

To complete each folded triangle, fold right top layer under, aligning bottom edge with center fold; secure fold with double-sided tape (Fig.1). Repeat with left top layer (Fig. 2). This creates a square fold on this side. Flip folded piece over, fold back right outside edge up and toward center fold, aligning back right outside edge with center fold (Fig. 3). Repeat with back left side (Fig. 4 and 5).

To assemble folded medallion, apply a small piece of double-sided tape to each folded piece in area shaded gray on Fig. 5. Referring to Fig. 6 with square side facing up, slip square on piece 1 under square on piece 2. Continue working around until medallion is complete (Fig. 7 and 8). To secure, adhere a 2-inch piece of white card stock or printed paper to back of medallion.

Adhere medallion to card front as shown. ∎

Sources: Linen card stock from The Japanese Paper Place; Chiyogami printed paper from Michaels Stores Inc.; stamp from Inkadinkado; distress ink pad from Ranger Industries Inc.; Apron Lace border punch from Fiskars.

Materials
- Card stock: light teal linen, white
- Teal/white floral Chiyogami printed paper
- "happy birthday" stamp
- Teal distress ink pad
- 16 inches ⅜-inch-wide sheer decorative ribbon
- Apron Lace border punch
- Double-sided tape
- Paper adhesive

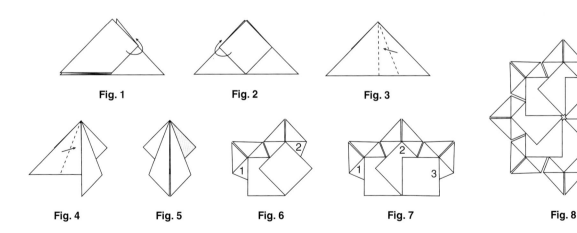

Fig. 1   **Fig. 2**   **Fig. 3**   **Fig. 4**   **Fig. 5**   **Fig. 6**   **Fig. 7**   **Fig. 8**

Dad, My Friend

Project note: *Use paper adhesive throughout unless otherwise instructed.*

Form a 5½ x 4¼-inch top-folded card from brown card stock. Emboss dots onto card front.

Cut twelve 1½-inch squares from polka-dot paper. Fold each square referring to Basic Triangle Fold instructions on page 5.

To complete each folded triangle, fold right top layer under, aligning bottom edge with center fold (Fig.1). Repeat with left top layer (Fig. 2). This creates a square fold on this side.

To assemble a square medallion, apply a small piece of double-sided tape to back right corner of square on each folded triangle. Slip bottom left layer of one folded piece under top layer of another folded piece, square side facing up (Fig. 3). Continue working around until medallion is complete (Fig. 4 and 5). Repeat process with remaining eight folded pieces, creating two more square medallions. Pierce a hole through center of each square medallion. Insert brads.

Using 1⅜-inch Labels One die template, die-cut four labels from ivory pearlescent card stock; set one label aside. Adhere a square medallion to each remaining die-cut label. Adhere to card front as shown using foam tape on center square medallion.

Cut a 6½ x ½-inch strip from polka-dot paper. Adhere strip to card front, ⅝ inch above bottom edge. Wrap ends inside card and secure. Cut set-aside die-cut label in half; adhere over ends of polka-dot strip inside card, aligning straight edges with outer edges of card front.

Stamp "dad" and "friend" onto ivory pearlescent card stock; cut out. Adhere to card front as shown. ∎

Sources: Chiyogami printed paper from The Japanese Paper Place; Family and Friends Word Stamps from Magnetic Poetry; chalk ink pad from Clearsnap Inc.; die templates from Spellbinders™ Paper Arts; embossing folders set, and die-cutting and embossing machine from Sizzix.

Materials
- Card stock: brown, ivory pearlescent
- Brown/ivory polka-dot Chiyogami printed paper
- Stamps: "dad," "friend"
- Light brown chalk ink pad
- 3 small antique copper brads
- Labels One die templates (#S4-161)
- Dots and Flowers Set embossing folders (#655838)
- Die-cutting and embossing machine
- Paper piercer
- Adhesive foam tape
- Double-sided tape
- Paper adhesive

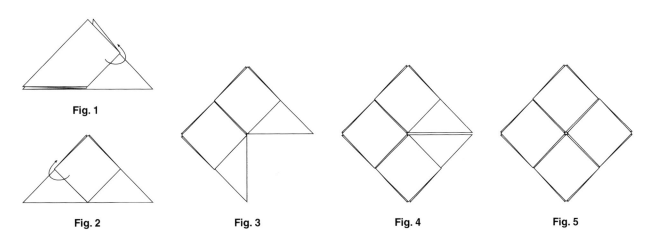

Fig. 1

Fig. 2

Fig. 3

Fig. 4

Fig. 5

Best Wishes

Project note: *Use paper adhesive throughout unless otherwise instructed.*

Card

Form a 5½ x 5⅜-inch side-folded card from Wash Board card stock. Adhere a 3 x 5⅜-inch piece of dark blue card stock to card front ⅛ inch from right edge.

Using desired embossing folder from Plum Blossom Set, emboss a 2½ x 5⅜-inch piece of Wash Board card stock, whitewash faceup. Lightly sand raised area. Adhere to card front as shown.

Cut a 4 x ¾-inch piece of Wash Board card stock. Place into embossing folder whitewash faceup, align with desired sentiment; emboss. Lightly sand raised portion. Ink edges of panel. Adhere to card front as shown.

Stamp Cloisonné Circle onto pale green paper six times. Using 2-inch circle punch, punch a circle from each stamped circle. Fold each circle referring to Basic Circle Fold instructions on page 6.

To complete each folded circle, refer to instructions and Fig. 1 and Fig. 2 from Love card on page 11.

To assemble a fan, apply a small piece of double-sided tape to back right of one folded piece. Slip bottom left layer of one folded piece under top layer of another folded piece (Fig. 1). Repeat with remaining folded pieces to create a total of three fans.

Using ⅝-inch punch, punch six circles from dark blue card stock. Adhere and sandwich a point of a folded fan between two ⅝-inch circles. Repeat with remaining fans. Adhere fans to card front as shown.

Tag

Emboss a 2 x 5-inch piece of White Board card stock whitewash side faceup. Lightly sand raised area. Adhere a ½ x 5-inch piece of dark blue card stock to side of embossed piece as shown.

In the same manner as for card, stamp Cloisonné Circle onto pale green paper three times; punch out each with 2-inch punch.

Fold each circle in the same manner as card circles.

Punch six ⅝-inch circles from dark blue card stock. Adhere and sandwich a point of a folded piece between two ⅝-inch circles. Repeat with remaining folded pieces. Adhere to tag as shown. ■

Sources: Whitewash Wash Board card stock from Core'dinations; stamp from Michael Strong Rubber Stamps; distress ink pad from Ranger Industries Inc.; 2-inch circle punch from Marvy Uchida; ⅝-inch circle punch from EK Success; Cuttlebug Plum Blossom Set embossing folders from Provo Craft; General Greetings embossing folder from Crafts-Too; embossing machine from Sizzix.

Materials
- Card stock: Whitewash Wash Board, dark blue
- Pale green paper
- Cloisonné Circle stamp
- Blue distress ink pad
- Circle punches: 2-inch, ⅝-inch
- Embossing folders: Plum Blossom Set (#20-00236); General Greetings (#CTFD3017)
- Embossing machine
- Sandpaper or sanding block
- Adhesive foam tape
- Double-sided tape
- Paper adhesive

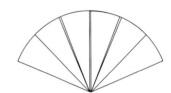

Fig. 1

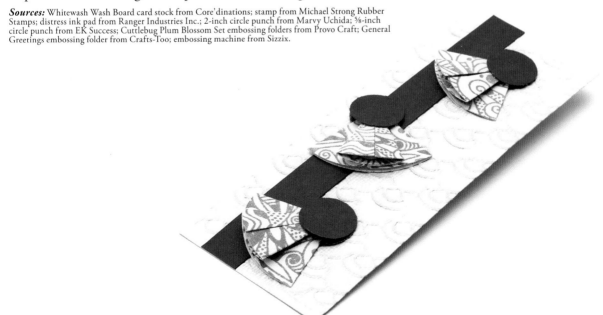

Congratulations

Project notes: Use paper adhesive throughout unless otherwise instructed. This medallion consists of a double fold, whereby the front and back of each piece is folded.

Card

Form a 5½ x 4¼-inch top-folded card from cream card stock. Emboss flowers onto card front and back. Adhere a 1½ x 4¼-inch piece of printed paper to card front as shown.

Apply ink to stamp, stamp image once onto scrap paper, then onto smooth side of cream card stock. *Note: Stamping onto scrap paper first will create a lighter image on sentiment panel.* Cut around sentiment and adhere to gray pearlescent paper; trim a small border. Adhere to lower left corner of card front.

Using 3⅜-inch Lacey Circles die template, die-cut and emboss a lacey circle from gray pearlescent paper. Adhere to card front as shown.

Cut eight 2-inch squares from printed paper. Fold each square referring to Basic Triangle Fold instructions on page 5.

To complete each folded triangle, fold left top layer under, aligning bottom edge with center fold; secure fold with double-sided tape (Fig.1). Repeat with right top layer (Fig. 2). This creates a square fold on this side. Fold left outside edge on bottom layer back toward center fold, aligning left outside edge to center fold; secure with double-sided tape (Fig. 3). Repeat with right side (Fig. 4). Fold left top edge down (Fig. 5).

To assemble folded medallion, apply a small piece of double-sided tape to back right corner of square on each folded piece. Slip bottom right layer of one folded piece under top layer of another folded piece, square side facing up (Fig. 6). Continue working around until medallion is completed (Fig. 7 and 8). Insert small crystal brad through center of medallion, piercing a hole if needed. Center and adhere to gray lacey circle on card front. ∎

Sources: Chiyogami printed paper from The Japanese Paper Place; stamp from MSE!; Lacey Circles die templates from Spellbinders™ Paper Arts; embossing folder, and die-cutting and embossing machine from Sizzix.

Materials
- Cream card stock
- Silver metallic Chiyogami printed paper
- Gray pearlescent paper
- "Congratulations!" stamp (#CC102)
- Gray dye ink pad
- 1 small crystal brad
- 1-inch circle punch
- Lacey Circles die templates (#S4-293)
- Tag Alongs die set (#37-1629)
- Dots and Flowers Set embossing folders (#655838)
- Die-cutting and embossing machine
- Piercing tool
- Double-sided tape
- Paper adhesive

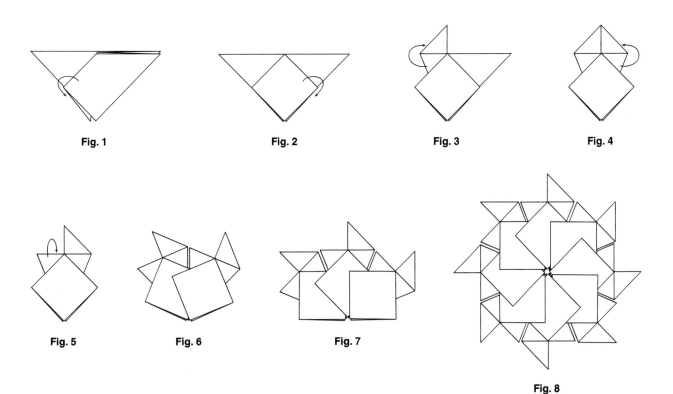

Fig. 1   Fig. 2   Fig. 3   Fig. 4

Fig. 5   Fig. 6   Fig. 7

Fig. 8

Celebrate

Project notes: *Use paper adhesive throughout unless otherwise instructed. This medallion consists of a double fold, whereby the front and back of each piece is folded.*

Form an 8½ x 4-inch top-folded card from navy blue card stock.

Cut an 8½ x 2-inch piece from red card stock and an 8½ x 2½-inch piece from white card stock. Layer and adhere pieces to card front as shown.

Stamp "Celebrate" onto white card stock; sprinkle with embossing powder and heat-emboss using embossing heat tool. Trim around sentiment; adhere to lower right corner of card front.

Cut 18 (1½-inch) squares from printed paper. Fold each square referring to Basic Triangle Fold instructions on page 5.

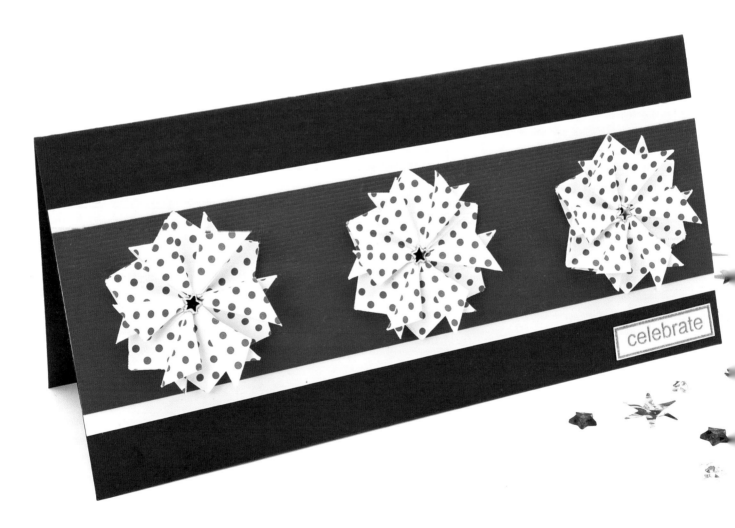

To complete each folded triangle, fold right top layer under, aligning bottom edge with center fold; secure fold with double-sided tape (Fig.1). Repeat with left top layer (Fig. 2). This creates a square fold on this side. Flip folded piece over; fold both the left and right outside edges up and toward midpoint before center fold. This will resemble a tulip (Fig. 3 and 4).

To assemble medallion using six folded pieces, apply a small piece of double-sided tape to back right corner of square on each folded piece. Slip bottom left layer of one folded piece under top layer of another folded piece, aligning edges as shown (Fig. 5). Continue working around until medallion is complete (Fig. 6 and 7). Repeat with remaining 12 folded pieces to create a total of three medallions.

Insert a silver star brad through center of each medallion, piercing a hole if needed. Adhere medallions to card front as shown. ∎

Sources: Printed paper from Michaels Stores Inc.; Family and Friends Word Stamps from Magnetic Poetry.

Materials
- Card stock: navy blue, red, white
- White/red dot printed paper
- "Celebrate" stamp
- Watermark ink pad
- Silver embossing powder
- 3 silver star brads
- Embossing heat tool
- Piercing tool
- Double-sided tape
- Paper adhesive

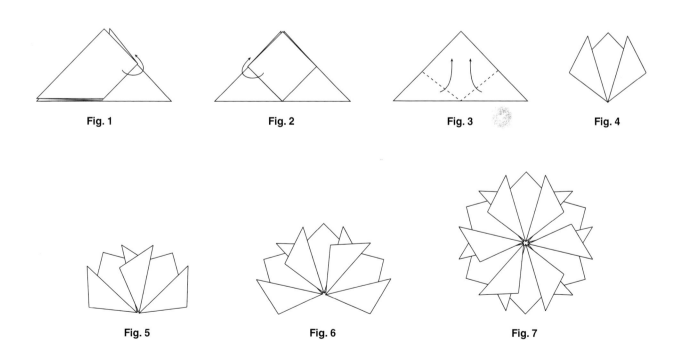

Fig. 1 Fig. 2 Fig. 3 Fig. 4

Fig. 5 Fig. 6 Fig. 7

Pocket Wishes

Materials

- Card stock: olive green, cream pearlescent
- Olive green/white dot Chiyogami printed paper
- White self-adhesive pearls: 1 medium, 6 small
- Cream satin heart
- Punches: Double Scallop Edger, 1½-inch circle
- Die templates: Standard Circles SM (#S4-116), Vintage Market Alphabet (#656623)
- Beautifully Boxed embossing folders (#37-1647)
- Die-cutting and embossing machine
- Bone folder
- Double-sided tape
- Paper adhesive
- Computer with printer (optional)

Project note: *Use paper adhesive throughout unless otherwise instructed.*

Card

Form a 4¼ x 5½-inch side-folded card from olive green card stock. Adhere a 4¼ x 1¾-inch strip of cream pearlescent card stock to top and bottom edges of card front.

Cut two 4¼ x 1¾-inch pieces from olive green card stock. Punch one long edge of each olive green strip using Double Scallop Edger punch. Adhere punched strips to top and bottom edges of card front, aligning straight edges as shown.

For pocket, cut a 3½ x 2½-inch piece from cream pearlescent card stock. Score a line ½ inch from each edge of cream pearlescent piece, leaving one short edge unscored. Trim corners of scored edges at an angle. Fold edges in along score lines; burnish creases with bone folder. Use 1½-inch circle punch to punch a half-circle from top unscored edge of pocket.

Cut a 3½ x ⅜-inch strip from printed paper. Wrap around cream pearlescent pocket ½ inch above bottom edge; secure ends of paper strip to back of pocket.

Adhere pocket to a 3 x 3⅜-inch piece of olive green card stock as shown, applying adhesive to folded edges of pocket only. Center and adhere to a 3¼ x 3⅝-inch piece of cream pearlescent card stock. Adhere to card front.

Using Alphabet Die, die-cut an "H" and a "B" from olive green card stock. Adhere to pocket as shown. Attach satin heart between letters on pocket. Attach small self-adhesive pearls to letters as shown.

Using "Happy Birthday" gift embossing folder, emboss a piece of cream pearlescent card stock. Trim embossed piece down to 2⅜ x 1¾ inches. Adhere to a 2⅜ x 2⅛-inch piece of olive green card stock, aligning bottom edges. This creates a gift-box panel that will slide inside pocket on card front.

Using 1⅝-inch Standard Circles SM die template, die-cut three circles from printed paper. Referring to Basic Circle Fold instructions on page 6, fold each circle.

To complete each folded circle, fold top right layer under and toward center fold, aligning outside right edge with center fold (Fig. 1). Repeat fold with top left layer (Fig. 2). Repeat with all folded circles.

To assemble gift bow, apply piece of double-sided tape to back right corner of each folded circle. Slip bottom layer of one folded circle under top layer of another folded circle (Fig. 3). Continue working around until gift bow is complete (Fig. 4). Punch a 1½-inch circle from cream pearlescent card stock. Adhere gift bow to top half of cream pearlescent circle.

Attach gift bow to back top edge of gift box as shown. Attach a medium self-adhesive pearl to gift-box panel as shown. Slide gift-box panel into pocket on card front.

Cut a 2½ x 3¾-inch rectangle from cream pearlescent card stock. Die-cut a 1⅛-inch circle from printed paper; cut in half. Adhere half-circles to top and bottom edges of cream pearlescent rectangle aligning straight edges. Center and adhere inside card.

Tag

Cut a 3 x 3¼-inch piece from cream pearlescent card stock. Cut two 3 x ¾-inch strips from olive green card stock; punch one long edge on each strip. Adhere strips to top and bottom edges of tag as shown.

In the same manner as for card, create another gift bow from printed paper. Unfold top layers slightly for extra dimension. Adhere bow to center top of tag.

Cut a 5½ x ¾-inch strip from printed paper; fold in half along long edge. Adhere ends of strip to back of tag to create a hanger as shown. Punch a 1½-inch circle from cream pearlescent card stock; cut in half. Adhere one half-circle to center top on back of tag covering ends of strip. ∎

Sources: Card stock from ANW Crestwood/The Paper Company; Chiyogami printed paper from The Japanese Paper Place; Double Scallop Edger Punch from Martha Stewart Crafts; 1½-inch circle punch from Marvy Uchida; Standard Circles SM die templates from Spellbinders™ Paper Arts; Vintage Market Alphabet Die, and die-cutting and embossing machine from Sizzix; Cuttlebug embossing folders from Provo Craft.

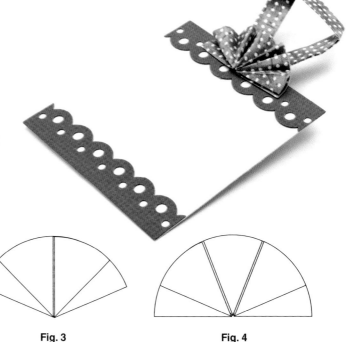

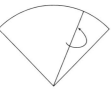
Fig. 1

Fig. 2

Fig. 3

Fig. 4

All the Best

Project note: *Use paper adhesive throughout unless otherwise instructed.*

Form a 5½ x 4¼-inch top-folded card from Mountain Meadow card stock. Adhere a 5½ x 1⅛-inch strip of mustard yellow card stock to card front, ⅞ inch above bottom edge.

Cut a 5½ x ½-inch strip of Mountain Meadow card stock; adhere across mustard yellow strip on card front as shown. Referring to photo, attach "ALL the Best" sticker to mustard yellow card-stock strip.

Using 2⅜-inch Classic Scalloped Circles SM die template, die-cut a scalloped circle from mustard yellow card stock. Adhere to lower right corner of card front.

Punch eight 2-inch circles from Brown Mini Plaid paper. Referring to Basic Circle Fold instructions on page 6, fold each circle. Apply double-sided tape to inside bottom layer to secure bottom layer of each circle.

To complete each folded circle, fold top right layer under and toward the center fold, aligning outside right edge with center fold (Fig. 1). Do not fold outside edge completely down; allow section to stick up for dimension. Repeat fold with top left layer (Fig. 2).

Materials

- Card stock: mustard yellow, light brown
- Back Country Mountain Meadow double-sided printed card stock
- Brown Mini Plaid printed paper
- Gold "ALL the Best" sticker
- Large mustard yellow brad
- 2-inch circle punch
- Classic Scalloped Circles SM die templates (#S4-125)
- Die-cutting machine
- Paper piercer
- Double-sided tape
- Paper adhesive

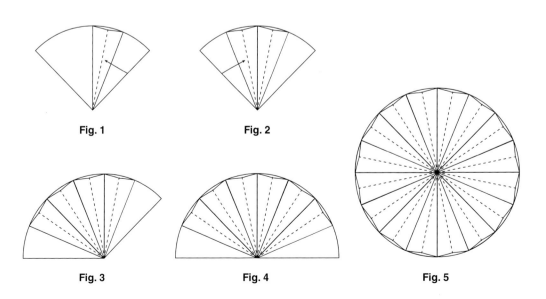

Fig. 1   Fig. 2

Fig. 3   Fig. 4   Fig. 5

To assemble rosette, apply double-sided tape to back left corner of each folded circle. Slip bottom layer of one folded circle under top layer of another folded circle (Fig. 3). Continue working around until rosette is completed (Fig. 4 and 5). To secure rosette, adhere it to a 2-inch circle punched from light brown card stock.

Using paper piercer, pierce a hole through middle of rosette; insert brad. Center and adhere rosette to mustard yellow scalloped circle on card. ■

Sources: Printed card stock from The Paper Loft; printed paper from Adornit; die templates from Spellbinders™ Paper Arts; die-cutting machine from Sizzix.

Falling Leaves

Project note: *Use paper adhesive throughout unless otherwise instructed.*

Card

Form a 4¼ x 5½-inch top-folded card from brown pearlescent card stock.

Adhere a 3¾ x 2⅜-inch piece of tan card stock to card front as shown.

Using leaf die template from Sunflower Set Two, die-cut a leaf from tan card stock. Leaving die template in place, ink die cut brown. Repeat using coral and white pearlescent card stock for a total of three inked leaves. Adhere leaves to card front as shown.

Cover corkboard or chipboard piece with printed paper; using cosmetic wedge, ink edges brown. Referring to photo, attach paper-covered panel to card front using foam tape.

Cut two 1½ x 1½-inch squares from brown pearlescent card stock and one from coral card stock. Adhere squares to card front as shown, using foam tape to adhere coral square.

Cut six 1½ x 1½-inch squares from floral paper. Fold each square referring to Basic Triangle Fold instructions on page 5.

To complete each folded triangle, fold right top layer under, aligning bottom edge with center fold (Fig. 1). Repeat with left top layer (Fig. 2). This creates a square fold on this side. Secure bottom layer of folded triangle and inside of folds on square fold with small pieces of double-sided tape.

To assemble half of the rosette, apply a piece of double-sided tape on back right side of each folded triangle. Slip taped side of one folded triangle under top layer of another folded triangle (Fig. 3). Continue with one more folded piece creating half of the rosette (Fig. 4). Repeat process with remaining three folded pieces.

Flip both half rosettes right side facedown. Aligning straight edges, secure half rosettes together with tape. Turn faceup; fold sides of squares up for dimension (Fig. 5). Adhere to coral square on card front as shown.

Tag

Using Embossed Tags embossing folder, die-cut and emboss a tag from brown pearlescent card stock.

In the same manner as for card, die-cut and ink leaves from tan, coral and white pearlescent card stock. Adhere to edge of tag as shown.

Referring to Fig. 1 and Fig. 2 folding instructions from card, create two folded pieces. Slide folded pieces onto corners of tag; adhere in place. ■

Sources: Card stock from ANW Crestwood/The Paper Company; Chiyogami printed paper from The Japanese Paper Place; stamp set from The Stamp Barn; chalk ink pad from Clearsnap Inc.; die templates from Spellbinders™ Paper Arts; Cuttlebug embossing folder from Provo Craft; die-cutting and embossing machine from Sizzix.

Materials

- Card stock: brown pearlescent, white pearlescent, tan, coral
- Leaves Chiyogami printed paper
- 2⅜ x 3¾-inch piece of corkboard or chipboard coaster
- Thinking of You stamp set (RSW011CU-lg)
- Brown chalk ink pad
- Sunflower Set Two die templates (#S4-158)
- Embossed Tags embossing folder (#20-00250)
- Die-cutting and embossing machine
- Cosmetic wedge
- Adhesive foam tape
- Double-sided tape
- Tape
- Paper adhesive

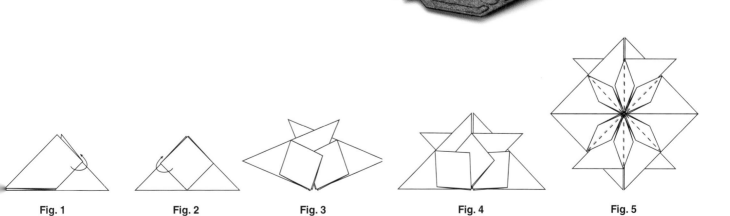

Fig. 1   Fig. 2   Fig. 3   Fig. 4   Fig. 5

Happy Halloween

Project note: *Use paper adhesive throughout unless otherwise instructed.*

Card

Form a 4¼ x 5½-inch side-folded card from dark purple card stock. Adhere a 3 x 5⅛-inch piece of Trick-Or-Treat paper to card front as shown.

Cut a 4¼ x 2-inch piece from sage green linen card stock; cut a piece of drywall tape the same size. Attach drywall tape piece on top of sage green piece. Pierce three holes through upper right corner of sage green piece; insert bat brads. Adhere to card front as shown.

Materials

- Card stock: dark purple, sage green linen, white, black
- Black linen text-weight paper
- Happy Halloween Trick-Or-Treat double-sided printed paper
- "happy Halloween" stamp
- Ink pads: black dye, metallic silver pigment
- Brads: 4 black bats, ½-inch square
- Tag Alongs die set (#37-1629)
- Die-cutting machine
- Cosmetic wedge
- Paper piercer
- Toothpick
- Drywall tape
- Adhesive foam tape
- Double-sided tape
- Paper adhesive

Using black ink, stamp "happy Halloween" onto smooth side of sage green linen card stock. Trim down to 1½ x 1⅛ inches. Using cosmetic wedge, ink edges black and metallic silver. Using foam tape, attach sentiment panel to lower right corner of Trick-Or-Treat paper piece on card front.

Cut eight 1¾-inch squares from black linen paper. Fold each square referring to Basic Triangle Fold instructions on page 5. Using cosmetic wedge, ink edges of each folded triangle metallic silver.

To assemble folded medallion, place a small piece of double-sided tape on back left corner of each folded triangle. Slip top layer of one folded triangle under top layer of another folded triangle (Fig. 1). Referring to Fig. 2–3, continue working around until medallion is complete.

Referring to Fig. 3 and Squash Fold instructions on page 7, squash-fold one corner of each triangle.

Cut a ½-inch square from sage green linen card stock; adhere to square brad. Insert square brad into center of medallion. Adhere medallion to card front as shown.

Tag

Using Tag Alongs die set, die-cut a tag from dark purple card stock.

Attach a 2 x 1¾-inch piece of drywall tape to tag ¼ inch above bottom edge. Cut a 2 x ¾-inch strip from Trick-Or-Treat paper, adhere to tag as shown. Referring to photo, adhere a 1¼ x 1¼-inch piece of sage green linen card stock to tag as shown.

Cut two 1¾ x 1¾-inch squares from black linen paper. Fold each triangle referring to Basic Triangle Fold instructions on page 5. Ink edges of each folded triangle metallic silver.

To assemble bat, apply a small piece of double-sided tape to back left corner on one triangle. Referring to Fig. 1, slip top layer of triangle without taped back under top layer of other folded triangle. Referring to Squash Fold instructions on page 7, squash-fold a corner of each folded triangle as shown in photo.

Adhere bat to tag as shown. Pierce a hole through upper right corner of tag and insert bat brad. ∎

Sources: Linen card stock from The Japanese Paper Place; printed paper from Echo Park Paper Co.; stamp from Hampton Art; brads from Making Memories; Cuttlebug die set from Provo Craft; die-cutting machine from Sizzix.

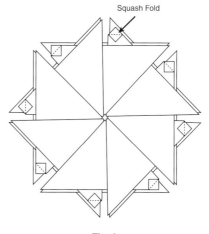

Squash Fold

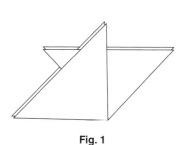

Fig. 1

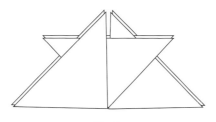

Fig. 2

Fig. 3

Elegant Thanks

Project note: *Use paper adhesive throughout unless otherwise instructed.*

Card

Form a 5½ x 5½-inch side-folded card from black card stock. Adhere a 3½ x 5½-inch piece of floral paper to card front as shown.

Using 2½-inch Lacey Squares die template, die-cut a lacey square from black card stock. Adhere to a 2½ x 2½-inch piece of turquoise pearlescent card stock.

Using embossing folder, emboss a piece of plum metallic paper. Trim embossed piece down to a 2 x 2-inch square. Adhere to black lacey square. Attach to card front as shown using foam tape.

Cut two 1½ x 1½-inch squares from floral paper. Fold both squares referring to Basic Square Fold instructions on page 6. Secure inside folds with double-sided tape. Set squares aside.

Materials
- Card stock: black linen, turquoise pearlescent, turquoise
- Blue/purple floral Chiyogami printed paper
- Plum metallic Midare paper
- Lacey Squares die templates (#S4-295)
- Thanks embossing folder (#37-1134)
- Die-cutting and embossing machine
- Toothpick
- Adhesive foam tape
- Double-sided tape
- Paper adhesive

Cut four 1½ x 1½-inch squares from plum metallic paper. Fold each square referring to Basic Triangle Fold instructions on page 5. To complete folded triangles, fold top left layer under and toward center fold, aligning outside left edge with center fold (Fig. 1). Repeat fold with top right layer (Fig. 2). Repeat with all folded triangles.

Referring to Fig. 3–5, and Squash Fold instructions on page 7, squash-fold both top corners on folded top layer of each triangle.

To assemble medallion, adhere a folded triangle under left and right sides of a folded floral square (Fig. 6 and 7). Repeat for second medallion. Adhere to card front as shown.

Tag

Die-cut a 2½ x 2½-inch lacey square from black card stock. Adhere a 2 x 2-inch piece of plum metallic paper to lacey square.

Create one medallion in the same manner as for card. Adhere to a 1½ x 1½-inch piece of floral paper, aligning outside straight edges. Adhere centered to tag. ∎

Sources: Linen card stock, Chiyogami paper and Midare paper from The Japanese Paper Place; templates from Spellbinders™ Paper Arts; Cuttlebug embossing folder from Provo Craft; die-cutting and embossing machine from Sizzix.

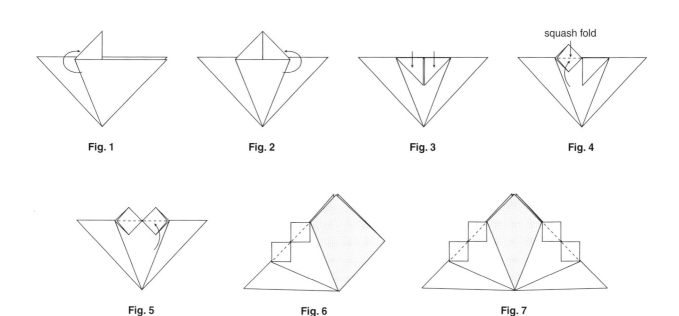

squash fold

Fig. 1   **Fig. 2**   **Fig. 3**   **Fig. 4**

Fig. 5   **Fig. 6**   **Fig. 7**

Paper Treat

Project note: *Use paper adhesive throughout unless otherwise instructed.*

Cut an 8½ x 5½-inch piece from orange card stock. With long edge horizontal, score a vertical line 2⅛ inches from both left and right sides. Fold flaps toward center to form a 4¼ x 5½-inch gatefold card.

Cut two ¾ x 5½-inch pieces from black card stock. Using Apron Lace border punch, punch one long edge of each black strip. *Note: Start first punch in center, and then align with drawings on punch to complete, referring to manufacturer's instructions.* Adhere a strip to each side of card front as shown.

Materials

- Card stock: orange, black, white
- Orange/white dot printed paper
- Copper metallic thread
- White brad
- Punches: Apron Lace border, 1½-inch circle
- Classic Scalloped Circles SM die templates (#S4-125)
- Dots and Flowers Set embossing folders (#655838)
- Die-cutting and embossing machine
- Scoring tool
- Clear tape
- Adhesive foam tape
- Double-sided tape
- Paper adhesive

Punch eight 1½-inch circles from printed paper. Referring to Basic Circle Fold instructions on page 6, fold each circle.

To assemble folded medallion, apply a small piece of double-sided tape to back left corner of each folded piece. Slip top layer of one folded triangle under top layer of another folded triangle (Fig. 1). Continue working around until circle is complete (Fig. 2 and 3). For added dimension, gently fold top layer of each folded triangle toward left side. Insert white brad through center hole of assembled medallion.

Using 2⅜-inch Classic Scalloped Circles SM die template, die-cut three scalloped circles, two from white card stock and one from black card stock.

Using dots embossing folder, emboss both white scalloped circles. Adhere embossed scalloped circles to right card flap, ⅜ inch below top edge and ⅜ inch above bottom edge.

Working from spool of copper metallic thread, use clear tape to adhere end of thread to center back of black scalloped circle. Referring to Fig. 4, wrap thread across front and in between seventh and eighth scallops to the right from starting point. Continue wrapping clockwise in this manner until two threads have been wrapped between each scallop. Punch a 1½-inch circle from black card stock, adhere to back of thread-wrapped scalloped circle.

Center and adhere medallion to thread-wrapped scalloped circle. Using foam tape, adhere to card front as shown. ***Note:*** *Make sure foam tape is not visible when card is open.* ∎

Sources: Printed paper from Michaels Stores Inc.; metallic thread from Wonderfil Threads; die templates from Spellbinders™ Paper Arts; Apron Lace border punch from Fiskars; 1½-inch circle punch from Marvy Uchida; embossing folders, and die-cutting and embossing machine from Sizzix.

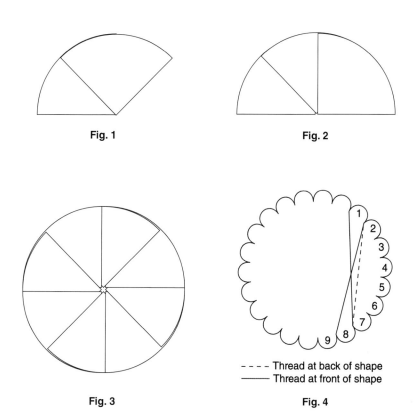

Fig. 1 Fig. 2

Fig. 3

- - - - Thread at back of shape
——— Thread at front of shape

Fig. 4

Season's Greetings

Project note: *Use paper adhesive throughout unless otherwise instructed.*

Form a 5½ x 5½-inch top-folded card from olive green card stock.

Cut eight 2-inch squares from printed paper. Fold each square referring to Basic Square Fold instructions on page 6. Apply double-sided tape to inside bottom layer to secure bottom layer of each square.

To complete each folded square, roll top right layer under and toward center fold; repeat with left top layer (Fig. 1). **Note:** *Refer to photo when rolling top layer toward center fold.*

To assemble folded medallion, apply double-sided tape to back left corner of each folded square. Slip bottom layer of one folded square under top layer of another folded square (Fig. 2). Continue working around until medallion is completed (Fig. 3 and 4). Attach gem to center of snowflake brad. Insert brad through center hole of assembled medallion.

Cut a 2½ x 2½-inch square from gold pearlescent card stock; using cosmetic wedge, lightly ink red. Center and adhere medallion to gold square. Adhere to a 2¾ x 2¾-inch piece of red card stock. Adhere to card front as shown.

Emboss "Season's Greetings" onto gold pearlescent card stock. Cut out. Adhere to a 4⅜ x 1-inch piece of red card stock. Adhere below medallion on card front. ∎

Sources: *Chiyogami printed paper from The Japanese Paper Place; pigment ink pad from Tsukineko LLC; Cuttlebug embossing folder from Provo Craft; die-cutting and embossing machine from Sizzix.*

Materials

- Card stock: olive green linen, gold pearlescent, red
- Red/green/gold metallic Chiyogami printed paper (#623C)
- Dark red pearlescent pigment ink pad
- Gold snowflake brad
- Red self-adhesive gem
- Season's Greetings embossing folder (#37-1931)
- Die-cutting and embossing machine
- Cosmetic wedge
- Double-sided tape
- Paper adhesive

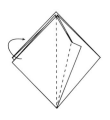

Fig. 1

Fig. 2

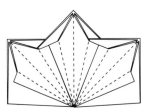

Fig. 3

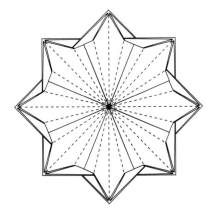

Fig. 4

Let It Snow

Project note: *Use paper adhesive throughout unless otherwise instructed.*

Card

Form a 5½ x 5½-inch side-folded card from printed paper. Punch right edge of card front with Apron Lace border punch.

Using Lacey Circles die template, die-cut and emboss a 2¾-inch lacey circle from turquoise card stock and a 2-inch lacey circle from lavender pearlescent card stock.

Using snowflake dies, die-cut a variety of snowflakes from white pearlescent card stock and turquoise card stock.

Layer and adhere snowflakes and die-cut lacey circles onto card front as shown using foam tape as desired.

Stamp "let it snow" onto turquoise card stock with watermark ink. Sprinkle with embossing powder, heat-emboss using embossing heat tool. Die-cut and emboss sentiment using smallest Beaded Circles die template. Adhere to lower right corner of card front.

Using blue ink, stamp Snowflake Inchie eight times onto white pearlescent text-weight paper; heat-set using embossing heat tool. Cut out each square. Referring to Basic Square Fold instructions on page 6, fold each square.

To assemble rosettes, apply a piece of double-sided tape to back left corner of eight folded squares. Slip top layer of one folded square under top layer of another folded square (Fig. 1). Referring to Fig. 2 and Fig. 3, continue working around until rosette is complete.

Materials

- Card stock: lavender pearlescent, white pearlescent, turquoise
- Winter Joy Stripe printed paper
- White pearlescent text-weight paper
- Stamps: "let it snow," Snowflake Inchie set
- Ink pads: watermark, blue distress
- Purple embossing powder
- Turquoise self-adhesive gem
- 2 lavender gemstone brads
- Apron Lace border punch
- Die templates: Lacey Circles (#S4-293), Beaded Circles (#S4-292), various snowflakes
- Die-cutting and embossing machine
- Embossing heat tool
- Adhesive foam tape
- Double-sided tape
- Paper adhesive

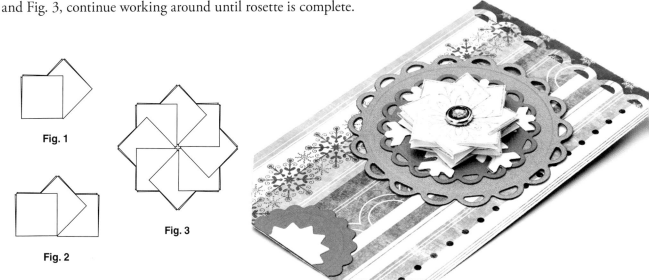

Fig. 1

Fig. 2

Fig. 3

Insert lavender gemstone brad through center of rosette. Adhere to card front as shown. Attach gem to snowflake as shown.

Tag

Cut a 3 x 4⅞-inch piece from printed paper. Referring to photo, trim corners on one short edge at an angle. Punch opposite short edge using Apron Lace border punch. Adhere a 3 x 1⅝-inch strip of printed paper to back edge of tag, extending past punched edge.

Die-cut a 2¾-inch lacey circle from lavender pearlescent card stock and a 2-inch lacey circle from turquoise card stock.

Die-cut two snowflakes from white pearlescent card stock. Layer and adhere lacey circles and one snowflake to tag as shown.

Die-cut a small beaded circle from turquoise card stock. Adhere remaining snowflake to beaded circle. Adhere to center of short trimmed edge, extending past edge. Trim die cuts flush to tag's edge.

Create a rosette in the same manner as card rosette. Insert brad through center of rosette; adhere to tag as shown. ■

Sources: Card stock from ANW Crestwood/The Paper Company; printed paper from Bo-Bunny Press; stamp set from Inkadinkado; distress ink pad from Ranger Industries Inc.; punch from Fiskars; die templates from Spellbinders™ Paper Arts; die-cutting and embossing machine from Sizzix.

Joy to You

Project note: *Use paper adhesive throughout unless otherwise instructed.*

Form a 5½ x 4¼-inch top-folded card from cream pearlescent card stock. Using embossing folder, emboss card leaving 1½ inches on right edge outside embossing folder.

Using Pinking Circles SM die templates, die-cut from pearlescent green paper three 1½-inch circles, three 2-inch circles and two 2½-inch circles.

Stamp sentiment onto bottom section of one 2½-inch die-cut circle. Sprinkle with embossing powder and heat-emboss using embossing heat tool. Adhere to top of card front as shown, folding top edge of sentiment circle over top edge of card front and securing to back.

Referring to Basic Circle Fold instructions on page 6, fold remaining die-cut circles.

Materials

- Pearlescent card stock:
  cream, brown
- Dark green pearlescent
  text-weight paper
- Gold Outline Stickers sheet (#1034)
- Joy to you & yours stamp
- Watermark ink pad
- Gold embossing powder
- ¼-inch star punch
- Pinking Circles SM die templates
  (#S4-172)
- Swiss Dots embossing folder
  (#37-1604)
- Die-cutting and embossing machine
- Embossing heat tool
- Straight pin
- Double-sided tape
- Paper adhesive

To complete each folded circle, fold top right layer under and toward center fold, aligning outside right edge with center fold (Fig. 1). Repeat fold with top left layer (Fig. 2). Repeat with all folded circles.

To assemble small tree, slide folded 2-inch piece into center fold of a 1½-inch folded piece (Fig. 3). Repeat to create second small tree.

For large tree, repeat small tree process, then slide remaining 2½-inch folded piece into center fold of 2-inch folded piece (Fig. 4).

Hand-cut three trunks for trees from brown card stock. Layer and adhere tree trunks and tree to card front as shown.

To decorate trees, remove small squares from peel-off sticker sheet using a straight pin. **Note:** *These are the pieces that usually remain on liner sheet once decorative sticker has been used.* Attach stickers to trees and card front as desired. Using star punch, punch three stars from border on stickers sheet; attach a star to top of each tree. ■

Sources: Card stock from ANW Crestwood/The Paper Company; Gold Outline Stickers from Starform; stamp from Impression Obsession; star punch from Fiskars; die templates from Spellbinders™ Paper Arts; Cuttlebug embossing folder from Provo Craft; die-cutting and embossing machine from Sizzix.

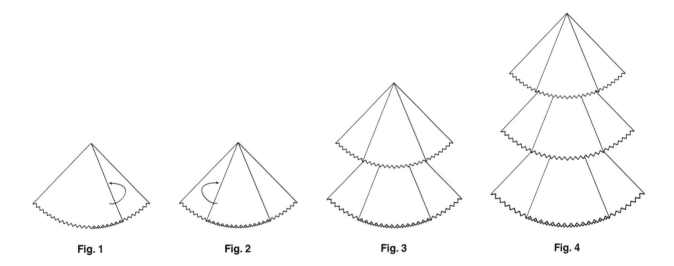

Fig. 1   Fig. 2   Fig. 3   Fig. 4

Happy New Year

Project note: *Use paper adhesive throughout unless otherwise instructed.*

Card

Form a 5½ x 4¼-inch side-folded card from navy blue card stock. With long edge horizontal on work surface, score a vertical line 2¾ inches from right edge of card front. Fold card front back along scored line forming an accordion-folded card. Using embossing folder, emboss front card flap.

Cut a 4½ x 3¼-inch piece from printed paper. Adhere to reverse side of front card flap as shown. Stamp "HAPPY New Year" onto navy blue card

stock. Sprinkle with embossing powder and heat-emboss using embossing heat tool. Cut a 3⅛ x 1¼-inch rectangle around sentiment. Adhere to card front as shown.

Cut three 1½ x 1½-inch squares from printed paper. Referring to Basic Square Fold instructions on page 6, fold each square. Complete folding by folding top layers of folded square upward (Fig. 1 and 2). Secure back layer using double-sided tape.

To assemble a half-medallion, slide bottom layer of one folded square onto bottom layer of another folded square and secure with double-sided tape (Fig. 3). Repeat with remaining folded piece (Fig. 4). *Note: Try something different with this medallion, assemble referring to Figures or photos. Top layer of center fold square can overlap the side folded squares (refer to tag photo) or edges of all three folded squares can be popped up (refer to card photo).* Adhere to card front as shown.

Tag
Using Tag Alongs die set, die-cut a tag from navy blue card stock. Emboss with embossing folder.

Create two half-medallions following instructions from card. Adhere to tag as shown. ■

Sources: Card stock from ANW Crestwood/The Paper Company; printed paper from Reminisce; stamp set from Papertrey Ink; Cuttlebug die set and embossing folder from Provo Craft; die-cutting and embossing machine from Sizzix.

Materials
- Navy blue pearlescent card stock
- Graduation Silver Swirl printed paper
- Communiqué Curves stamp set
- Watermark ink pad
- Silver embossing powder
- Tag Alongs die set (#37-1629)
- D'vine Swirl embossing folder (#37-1142)
- Die-cutting and embossing machine
- Embossing heat tool
- Scoring tool
- Double-sided tape
- Paper adhesive

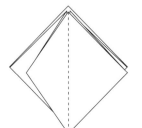

Fig. 1

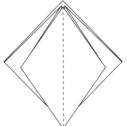

Fig. 2

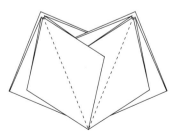

Fig. 3

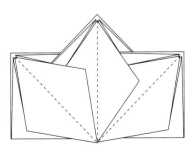

Fig. 4

Love Notes

Project note: Use paper adhesive throughout unless otherwise instructed.

Card

Cut an 8½ x 5½-inch piece from cream pearlescent card stock. With long edge horizontal, score vertical lines 2⅛ inches from both left and right sides. Fold flaps toward center to form a 4¼ x 5½-inch gatefold card. Adhere a 2 x 5⅜-inch piece of printed paper to each front panel.

Using embossing folder, emboss "LOVE" onto cream pearlescent card stock. Trim down to a 2½ x ⅞-inch piece. Center and adhere to card front adhering panel to left front panel only.

Using 2¾-inch Beaded Circles die template, die-cut and emboss two beaded circles from cream pearlescent card stock. Insert ends of ribbon through holes at center bottom of one beaded circle. Cross

Materials
- Cream pearlescent card stock
- Avignon Orchestra printed paper
- 3 inches ¼-inch-wide brown sheer ribbon
- 2 large pearl brads
- Die templates: Beaded Circles (#S4-292), Tag Alongs set (#37-1629)
- Love Is In The Air Set embossing folders (#20-00221)
- Die-cutting and embossing machine
- Scoring tool
- Double-sided tape
- Paper adhesive

ribbon ends over each other on back and insert ribbon ends through opposite holes to return to front. Trim ends at an angle. Center and adhere beaded circle with ribbon to card front adhering circle to right front panel only. Set remaining beaded circle aside.

Cut eight 1½ x 1½-inch squares from printed paper. Fold each square referring to Basic Square Fold instructions on page 6.

To complete each folded square, fold right top layer under, aligning outside bottom edge with center fold (Fig. 1). Repeat with left top layer (Fig. 2). Fold remaining squares in this manner.

To assemble rosette, place a small piece of double-sided tape on back right side of each folded piece. Slip taped side of one folded piece under top layer of another folded piece (Fig. 3). Continue working around until rosette is complete (Fig. 4 and 5).

Insert brad through center of rosette. Center and adhere to beaded circle.

Adhere a 3¾ x 2¾-inch piece of printed paper inside card. Center and adhere remaining beaded circle inside card.

Tag
Using Tag Alongs die set, die-cut a tag from cream pearlescent card stock.

Die-cut and emboss a small beaded circle from cream pearlescent card stock.

Adhere a 2 x 1½-inch piece of printed paper to tag. Cut die-cut circle in half and adhere to printed paper as shown.

Referring to card instructions, create four folded pieces. Referring to photo, adhere folded pieces together using tape. Insert brad through center of rosette. Adhere to tag. ∎

Sources: Card stock from ANW Crestwood/The Paper Company; printed paper from 7gypsies; Beaded Circles die templates from Spellbinders™ Paper Arts; Cuttlebug Tag Alongs die set and embossing folders from Provo Craft; die-cutting and embossing machine from Sizzix.

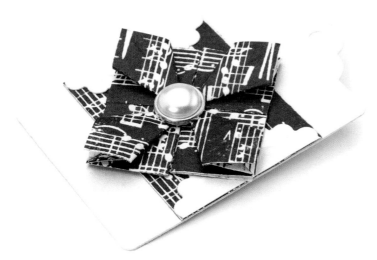

Fig. 1

Fig. 2

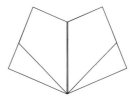

Fig. 3

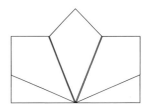

Fig. 4

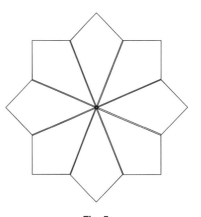

Fig. 5

Buyer's Guide

The Buyer's Guide listings are provided as a service to our readers and should not be considered an endorsement from this publication.

7gypsies
(877) 412-7467
www.sevengypsies.com

Adornit
(435) 563-1100
www.adornit.com

ANW Crestwood/The Paper Company
(973) 406-5000
www.anwcrestwood.com

Bazzill Basics Paper Inc.
(800) 560-1610
www.bazzillbasics.com

Bo-Bunny Press
(801) 771-4010
www.bobunny.com

Clearsnap Inc.
(800) 448-4862
www.clearsnap.com

Core'dinations
www.coredinations.com

Crafts-Too
www.crafts-too.com

Creative Imaginations
www.cigift.com

Echo Park Paper Co.
(800) 701-1115
www.echoparkpaper.com

EK Success
www.eksuccess.com

Fiskars
(866) 348-5661
www.fiskarscrafts.com

Hampton Art
(800) 981-5169
www.hamptonart.com

Impression Obsession
(877) 259-0905
www.impression-obsession.com

Inkadinkado
www.inkadinkado.com

The Japanese Paper Place
(416) 538-9669
www.japanesepaperplace.com

Magnetic Poetry
(800) 370-7697
www.magneticpoetry.com

Making Memories
(801) 294-0430
www.makingmemories.com

Martha Stewart Crafts
www.marthastewartcrafts.com

Marvy Uchida
(800) 541-5877
www.marvy.com

Memory Box
www.memoryboxco.com

Michaels Stores Inc.
(800) MICHAELS (642-4253)
www.michaels.com

Michael Strong Rubber Stamps
www.strongstamps.com

MSE!
(719) 260-6001
www.sentiments.com

The Paper Loft
(801) 254-1961
www.paperloft.com

Papertrey Ink
www.papertreyink.com

Penny Black Inc.
(800) 488-3669
www.pennyblackinc.com

Provo Craft
(800) 937-7686
www.provocraft.com

Ranger Industries Inc.
(732) 389-3535
www.rangerink.com

Reminisce
www.designsbyreminisce.com

Sizzix
(877) 355-4766
www.sizzix.com

Spellbinders™ Paper Arts
(888) 547-0400
www.spellbinderspaperarts.com

Stamp Barn
(800) 246-1142
www.stampbarn.com

Starform
www.starform.com

Tsukineko LLC
(425) 883-7733
www.tsukineko.com

Wonderfil Threads
(866) 250-6101
www.wonderfil.net